# Curls 3

### VERSATILE, WEARABLE

### WRAPS TO KNIT AT ANY GAUGE

## Hunter Hammersen

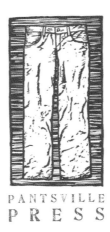

PANTSVILLE
PRESS

Charts created with Stitchmastery Knitting Chart Editor.

ISBN: 978-1-7325229-0-9

First Printing, 2018

Printed in China

Pantsville Press

Maine

www.pantsvillepress.com

# Contents

12

16

20

24

28

32

36

40

44

48

52

# Introduction

You know how I'm always telling you to swatch (really, if I could give only one piece of knitting advice, it would be to learn to love swatching)? Well this book (and the two that came before it) exists because of swatching!

I was getting to know a pretty little stitch pattern and experimenting with how to increase while maintaining the overall pattern. The shape I ended up with caught my eye. It was delightfully curvy and swirly and organic. That first swatch quickly led to another, and another, and another. Before I knew it, I had a stack of swatches and sketches and the start of a plan. Those swatches became the first Curls book. It was so much fun that I did it again for Curls 2, and now it seems I've done it one more time.

I call these pieces Curls because of their shape. They're gently curved on both the top and the bottom, and that means they drape beautifully around your neck and shoulders (there's a picture on the next page if you want to see what they look like laid out flat). It also means that they're amazingly flexible. Make them small and wear them like a cowl, or keep going and make a giant piece to wear as a scarf or a shawl. The shape makes them easy to wear, and they will sit beautifully no matter what size you make. And best of all, because the shape is so flexible, you can work with any weight of yarn, at any gauge, and make any size piece you please. They're just about the most adaptable, accommodating thing you can imagine!

The pieces in the book show off some of that flexibility. They're worked in light fingering, fingering, sport, and DK yarns (and they'd work just as well in lace weight or worsted weight yarn if you wanted to be even bolder). The smallest has a wingspan of 40 inches (which sits perfectly on your shoulders), and the largest clocks in at 72 inches (which is enough to wrap around yourself twice and keep you super cozy). One uses less than 500 yards of yarn, another uses more than 1,100 yards. But the best thing is that *any* of these patterns would work in *any* of the weights of yarn and look beautiful at *any* of the sizes. They really are magic!

Oh, and to make them even more fun, I've designed each of these Curls to work especially well with speckled or gradient yarns. I am absolutely helpless to resist these yarns, but sometimes it's hard to find just the right pattern for them. But all of these pieces were created with these special yarns in mind (though of course they will look great with regular yarn too).

All you need to do is pick a pattern, grab your favorite yarn, and cast on!

# Anatomy of a Curl

Before we dive in, let me say you can totally skip this part (though I do recommend you at least read the Hints section on page 6). It is officially allowed. You can turn to the patterns and dive right in, and everything will come out fine. That's half the fun of these projects. They just sort of work on their own! I will never know you skipped ahead, and your Curls will be lovely.

But if you do want to understand what's going on (either to modify the patterns provided here or to make up your own), this is the place to be.

I'll begin by taking you through the pieces of a Curl. Then I'll talk a bit about how a Curl comes together, how the charts are laid out, and some of the modifications you might see from one pattern to the next.

This diagram shows the five pieces of a Curl.

*The pictures on the facing page show two Curls, Lepidolite (top) and Rhodonite (bottom), spread out flat and oriented more or less the way you'd wear them. The bound off edge (section 5) is on the bottom. The increases (section 4) are on the top. The edge (section 1) is on the left or right.*

1 **EDGE** This section makes up the straight edge on one side of the Curl. It will be two or more stitches wide and will have as many rows as the main repeat.

2 **MAIN REPEAT** This section is the main attraction. It's the pattern that makes up the field of your Curl. It can be any size.

3 **WEDGE** This section prepares you for the next instance of the main repeat. Its size and shape are the most variable of all the pieces. It will have as many rows as the main repeat, and its width will be a multiple of the width of the main repeat. It will often incorporate parts of the stitch pattern found in the main repeat.

4 **INCREASES** This section lets your Curl grow. It gives you the new stitches the wedge needs. It will be a few stitches wide (and the stitch count may vary from row to row) and will be as tall as the main repeat.

5 **FINISH** This gets your stitches ready to bind off. Sometimes it's one row, sometimes it's several, and sometimes it's not there at all.

These five pieces, taken together, make up the most basic Curl. But if you just knit that, you'd have a tiny piece of fabric. The magic happens when you continue to repeat the edge, main repeat, wedge, and increases. Each time you repeat them, your knitting gets bigger, and it starts to form a lovely curved shape.

It all works because the wedge and the increases make room for more copies of the main repeat. That means that once you've worked through your edge, main repeat, wedge, and increases once, you've got the right number of stitches to work through them again, this time with one (or more) extra repeats of the main repeat.

This is so much easier to see with a diagram. This picture shows a series of edge, main repeat, wedge, and increases worked four times. See how the number of the main repeat increases? That's how your Curl grows.

Now to keep the charts to a reasonable size (and to prevent them from looking too daunting), they'll look more like the diagram on the previous page than like the one below. That is, they'll generally only show you one set of edge, main repeat, wedge, and increases sections (plus the finish if you need it). You'll just keep working the main repeat as needed until

the Curl is the size you want. And don't worry, the colors on the charts match up with what you're seeing here, and there's always a note with all the numbers you might need. Once you've got the stitches on your needles, I think you'll find the whole process very intuitive!

Part of the fun of Curls is their flexibility. While the principles outlined above hold for all Curls, there are lots of variations. I'd like to outline a few here just so you're not surprised when you come across them in the patterns.

Each individual pattern will have a little guide like the ones shown on the next page that maps out the shape and growth of that particular Curl.

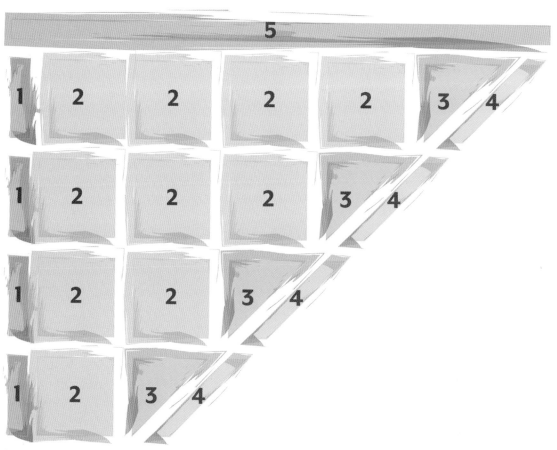

**FLIP THINGS AROUND** There's no reason the edge has to be on the left. It works just as well on the right. About half the patterns have the edge on the left and half on the right.

**START WITH A WEDGE** Often, especially if the main repeat is rather wide, there's not a good way to jump in with a main repeat right from the start. In those cases, you can start with a wedge and use it to create the space you need a little farther into the piece.

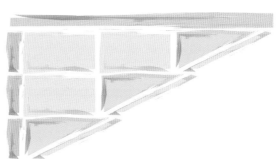

**LEAVE SOME PIECES OUT** Sometimes you don't need a special chart to be ready to bind off, and the pattern may not include a finish section.

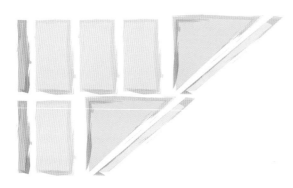

**CHANGE THE SLOPE** In the example we started with, there was room for one more main repeat every time you worked through the series of edge, main repeat, wedge, and increases. But that isn't set in stone. You can make space for two or three or even more extra main repeats each time. It all depends on how fast the Curl grows. Different rates of increase will give you different finished proportions.

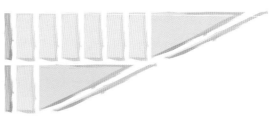

# Hints

**BLOCKING** See page 9.

**CAST ON** These cast ons are quite short, so you can use whatever cast on you like best. The projects here use the long-tailed cast on.

**CAST OFF** The bound-off edge needs to be very stretchy, I recommend Jeny's Surprisingly Stretchy Bind Off as seen in the Fall 2009 issue of *Knitty*. You're welcome to use another, but it is important to make sure it's stretchy!

**CHARTS** See page 8.

**GAUGE** See page 7.

**NEEDLES** See page 7.

**RIGHT-SIDE ROW** Right-side rows are worked with the public side of the Curl facing you. While you knit them, read the chart from right to left and follow the right-side notations in the stitch key. See page 8 for more.

**SIZING** See page 7.

**SLIPPED STITCHES** All of the projects call for slipping stitches along the edge of the knitting to create a tidy selvage edge. There are almost as many ways to do this as there are knitters. If you're getting elongated stitches along the edge of the fabric, you're doing it right!

One approach that works for most people is to always slip the first stitch as if to purl with your yarn held to the wrong side of the fabric. If you find that's not working for the way you knit, you can also try holding the yarn to the back of the work and slipping as if to knit on right-side rows and holding the yarn to the front of the work and slipping as if to purl on wrong-side rows.

**STITCH DEFINITIONS** Any unusual or potentially unknown stitches are defined as you encounter them. Look for the grey boxes with each pattern for the details of that pattern's fancy stitchwork.

**STITCH MARKERS** You may find it helpful to separate each instance of the main repeat with a stitch marker.

**SWATCHES** Swatches are always a good idea. Always. That said, these projects are unusually forgiving, and getting a particular gauge isn't important (as long as you like the fabric you're getting, see page 7 for more about this). If you wanted to just start knitting and judge your fabric once you're a few inches in, I won't tell.

**WINGSPAN** This is the edge created by the stitches you add when you work the increases. It is opposite the bound-off edge and will likely be closest to your neck when you wear your Curl.

**WRONG-SIDE ROW** Wrong-side rows are worked with the private side of the Curl facing you. While you knit them, read the chart from left to right and follow the wrong-side notations in the stitch key. See page 8 for more.

**YARN REQUIREMENTS** Each pattern lists a generous estimate for the yarn needed to complete the project *as shown in the picture*. This is a good guideline, but estimating yardage requirements is a bit of a black art. If you decide to make your Curl with a different weight of yarn or in a different finished size, you'll need a different amount of yarn. See page 7 for more about this. Luckily, these are perfect knit-until-the-yarn-runs-out projects!

# Gauge, Needles, & Sizing

One of the most marvelous things about Curls is their flexibility. You can use just about any weight of yarn, and you can make them in whatever size you'd like. That's wonderful, and it gives you a tremendous amount of freedom to create exactly what you want, but it does mean I can't tell you too much about your gauge, which needles to use, how big to make your Curl, or how much yarn you'll need.

Think about it for a moment. If I show you a Curl worn as a cowl and made with fingering-weight yarn, and you decide to knit that same Curl to wear as a shawl using a worsted-weight yarn, of course you're going to get a different gauge, use different needles, end up with a different size, and use a different number of yards of yarn. That's how it's *supposed* to work. These patterns give you the freedom to use whatever yarn you choose and to make whatever size you'd like.

I've listed the gauge for the samples shown in the book, but you don't need to worry about matching it. The most important thing to remember about gauge is that *if you're getting a fabric you like, you've got the right gauge*! If, as you work, you find you want a tighter, firmer fabric, go down a needle size. If you want a looser, drapier fabric, go up a needle size. You're in complete control.

The same applies for the size of your Curl. Have a small skein of yarn? Make a cowl. The smallest project shown here used just under 500 yards of yarn. And if you want to make a giant shawl to snuggle up in, you can do that too. You're in charge. If you're happy, it's perfect.

I do recommend checking the size of your Curl from time to time as they have been known to grow rather quickly. To do that, you're going to want to stretch it out to its full size. The edge with the live stitches wants to curve, so you need to get your stitches onto something flexible. If you're using circulars and your cable is long enough, you can use that (being careful not to let stitches pop off the ends). If not, a piece of waste yarn will do the trick. Just transfer your stitches to a piece of waste yarn, spread your Curl out flat, and see if you've got the size you like (go ahead and give it a good tug as most knitting grows a bit with blocking).

# Charts

I love charts. They're a great way to present a large amount of information in a small amount of space. But as much as I love them, I realize that they can seem a bit daunting if you're not used to them. Once you get to know them though, they're really not hard. The most important thing to remember is that charts show you a stylized picture of the right side of your work. Keep that in mind, and you're halfway there!

The easiest way to get to know a chart is to work through an example. So let's talk through this sample chart step by step.

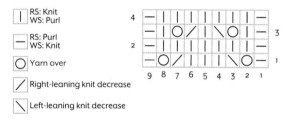

Always start with row 1, which is always the bottom row. First, figure out if row 1 is a right-side row or a wrong-side row. The instructions will tell you, but you can also tell from the chart. If it's a right-side row, the row number will be on the right of the chart. If it's a wrong-side row, the row number will be on the left of the chart.

*In this example, row 1 is a right-side row.*

Now start knitting! Just read across the chart and make the stitches in the order they're shown. Since you're working a right-side row, you'll work across the row from right to left and make the stitches as indicated by the right-side (RS) entries in the stitch key.

*Row 1: purl 1, yarn over, work a left-leaning knit decrease, knit 3, work a right-leaning knit decrease, yarn over, purl 1.*

Next, move on to row 2. All the patterns in this book are worked flat, so you'll always turn your work at the end of every row. Row 2 is a wrong-side row. Since you're working a wrong-side row, you'll work across the chart from left to right and make the stitches as indicated by the wrong-side (WS) entries in the stitch key. If a stitch doesn't have both RS and WS entries, it's either only worked on right-side rows, or it's the same on both right-side and wrong-side rows.

*Row 2: knit 1, purl 7, knit 1.*

Turn your work again, and move on to row 3, a right-side row.

*Row 3: purl 1, knit 1, yarn over, work a left-leaning knit decrease, knit 1, work a right-leaning knit decrease, yarn over, knit 1, purl 1.*

Turn your work again and move to row 4, a wrong-side row.

*Row 4: knit 1, purl 7, and knit 1.*

That's really all there is to it! Some charts are bigger, but the basic principles always hold.

The only other thing you might want to pay attention to is stitch repeats. These are indicated by heavy borders surrounding blocks of stitches. When you see these, you know you'll need to repeat the stitches within the borders as described in the stitch key and notes. You may want to separate stitch repeats with stitch markers to help you keep track of them.

# Blocking

Curls pop into shape with blocking. The pieces here have all been vigorously blocked, and you'll almost certainly want to do the same with yours.

Start by soaking your Curl in cool water for at least half an hour. Then, roll it up in a towel and gently squeeze out the excess water.

Unroll it, lay it out on your blocking surface (I use blocking mats, but a bed or even a clean carpet will work), and pat it into shape.

Your shape will look something like the swatches below or the pictures on page 2 though the precise shape will change depending on which pattern you're following.

You can block your Curl with pins or with a combination of pins and blocking wires. If you're using only pins, pin out the straight edge first (I use a ruler to keep it nice and even). Next, stretch the top edge (that's your

bound-off edge) and pin it in place. If you're using pins and blocking wires, start by threading your wires through the bound-off edge (I like to look for landmarks in the pattern repeat, for example a cable cross or a decrease, and always go through the same spot), then pin out the straight edge, and finally pin out the wires. In either case, be sure to use rust-proof pins.

Go ahead and give your work a good, firm tug as you're blocking to really open up your stitches. Depending on the pattern, the edge may have ripples or be smooth. You can emphasize any ripples by where you put your pins or run your wire.

Finally, let it dry completely (I know it's hard, but it's important) before carefully unpinning.

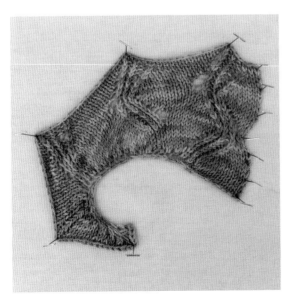

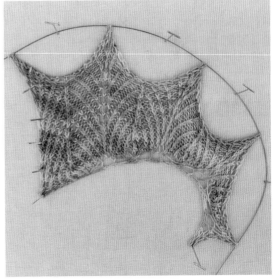

# Speckles & Gradients

I'm a fan of systems and categories. This makes me a challenging to live with (what do you mean you were unaware of the sock sorting scheme…those three baskets are obviously fancy hand knit socks, plain hand knit socks, and commercial socks…what could be clearer), but it means I had great fun thinking about speckles and gradients and the sorts of patterns I like best for each.

I've organized the patterns here into speckles (the first four), single-skein gradients (the next two), and multi-skein gradients (the last five) because that's how my brain works. But you should feel free to mix and match and experiment to find what you love best!

As a general guideline, single-skein gradients are the most accommodating yarns imaginable. You get all the excitement of their amazing colors, and the slow transitions mean you can use them without any extra work. Speckled yarns (like their cousins, highly variegated, multicolor yarns) are occasionally opinionated. But find a stitch pattern that lets them shine, and they are an absolute delight. And multi-skein gradients are pretty much the knitter's version of a new box of crayons…all those beautiful colors just waiting for you to play with them.

And remember, the yarn categories are just a guideline (someone is out there right now making a speckled gradient that will look amazing and fit in every category at once). You're the expert on your knitting, and if you like your fabric, you're absolutely doing it right!

**SPECKLES** The line between highly variegated, multicolor yarn and speckled yarn is sometimes blurry. But however you classify them, those hits of color are irresistible!

If a yarn has a clear background color with little bits of additional colors sprinkled on top, I call it a speckle (while if there's no one dominant background color, I call it a multi). Some speckles have tiny, sharply defined dots of color, and some have longer, softer edged bits of color.

I find speckles work best when you give the yarn plenty of room to do it's thing. Busy stitch patterns just get lost. I have much better luck with stitch patterns that use lots of stockinette (Indicolite), large-scale lace (Lepidolite, or Merlinite), or strong, straight lines (Howlite). The yarn is the star, let it shine!

**SINGLE-SKEIN GRADIENTS** Those hypnotic cakes? The ones that look like something from an astronomy magazine and you can't help but pick them up? Those are single-skein gradients!

I think of any yarn that makes a gradual transition from one color to another as a single-skein gradient. Some transition from light to dark shades of the same color, some move from one color to a second color, and some work through a several different colors.

Yarns like this are easy to work with. The color transitions are slow and smooth, so they don't distract from whatever else is going on with your pattern. You can totally use a single-skein gradient for just about any pattern (and any of the patterns in the first two Curls books would look great in a single-skein gradient).

I do recommend either getting two skeins of the gradient yarn and having one flow into the next (that's what I did with Charoite) or looking for a dyer who offers an extra skein of the first or last color of your skein (that's what I did with Chalcopyrite). Having that extra yarn will make sure you don't run short!

**MULTI-SKEIN GRADIENTS** I think of these as pre-approved color palettes for folks who are a little nervous about colors (that's totally me)!

If it's a set of related skeins, I call it a multi-skein gradient. Just like the single-skein gradients, they can move through different shades of the same color (like Apatite or Rhodonite) or move through different colors (like Zincite). And sometimes there's an accent color either included in the bundle (like Kyanite) or available separately (like Cacoxenite) to make things even more fun.

Because each skein is its own color, the transitions will be more distinct than with the single-skein gradients. That makes room for all sorts of fun variations on stripes. But it also means that it's a good idea to pay attention to how many different colors are in your bundle (I've given notes about the yarns I used so you can pick suitable yarns of your own). And don't be afraid of experimenting if you want to work with a different number of colors than the pattern calls for. Colored pencils can help with planning if you want to get creative (and they're way faster than swatching)!

Howlite

**SHOWN IN** Daintree, a fingering-weight yarn by Skein, in the color Seaview.

**GAUGE & SIZING** Shown at 32 stitches in 4 inches in pattern as charted. The piece shown used 725 yards of yarn and has a wingspan of 43 inches.

**CAST ON** Cast on 11 stitches.

**BODY** Odd rows are wrong-side rows. Even rows are right-side rows.

Work the Chart, repeating the 8 rows surrounded by the thick border as described in the key and note, until Curl reaches desired size. Each right-side row increases the stitch count by 3. Each wrong-side row increases the stitch count by 2 (except rows 7 & 14 which do not increase the stitch count). Stop after completing row 15 of the Chart (pay special attention here, you're not finishing the whole Chart, you're stopping after row 15).

Work the Finish Chart once. You'll repeat the 18 stitches surrounded by the purple border as needed to use up your stitches.

**FINISHING** Bind off loosely using a stretchy bind off. Weave in ends. Block to shape.

**NOTE** The 8 rows surrounded by the thick border are repeated to adjust the size of the Curl. The first time you work them, work the block of yellow stitches once. The second time you work them, work the block of yellow stitches 2 times. Each subsequent time you work them, work the block of yellow stitches 1 more time.

**LEFT-LEANING TWISTED KNIT DECREASE** Insert the right needle from the right to the left into the back loops of 2 stitches. Knit them together.

**CENTERED TWISTED DOUBLE KNIT DECREASE** Slip 1 as if to purl. Remount the next stitch so it is rotated 180 degrees (one half turn) clockwise. Return the slipped stitch to the left needle. Slip 2 together at the same time as if to knit 2 together. Knit 1. Pass the slipped stitches over.

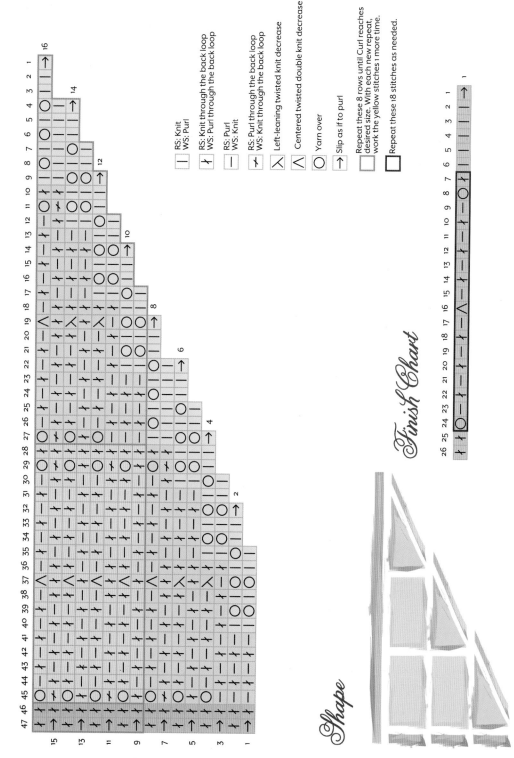

## Chart

**Legend:**

| | RS: Knit / WS: Purl |
| | RS: Knit through the back loop / WS: Purl through the back loop |
| | RS: Purl / WS: Knit |
| | RS: Purl through the back loop / WS: Knit through the back loop |
| | Left-leaning twisted knit decrease |
| | Centered twisted double knit decrease |
| O | Yarn over |
| ↑ | Slip as if to purl |
| ☐ | Repeat these 8 rows until Curl reaches desired size. With each new repeat, work the yellow stitches 1 more time. |
| ▢ | Repeat these 18 stitches as needed. |

## Finish Chart

## Shape

14

# Lepidolite

**SHOWN IN** Silky Victoria, a sport-weight yarn by Blue Moon Fiber Arts, in the color Sugar Plum Fairy Dust.

**GAUGE & SIZING** Shown at 22 stitches in 4 inches in pattern as charted. The piece shown used 650 yards of yarn and has a wingspan of 52 inches.

**CAST ON** Cast on 8 stitches.

**BODY** Odd rows are right-side rows. Even rows are wrong-side rows.

Work the Chart, repeating the 16 rows surrounded by the thick border as described in the key and note, until Curl reaches desired size. Each row increases the stitch count by 2. Stop after completing row 24 or 32 of the Chart.

Work a final row by slipping the first stitch as if to purl and knitting to the end.

**FINISHING** Bind off loosely using a stretchy bind off. Weave in ends. Block to shape.

**NOTE** The 16 rows surrounded by the thick border are repeated to adjust the size of the Curl. The first time you work them, work the block of yellow stitches once. The second time you work them, work the block of yellow stitches 2 times. Each subsequent time you work them, work the block of yellow stitches 1 more time.

**RIGHT-LEANING TWISTED KNIT DECREASE** Slip 1 as if to purl. Remount the next stitch so it is rotated 180 degrees (one half turn) clockwise. Return the slipped stitch to the left needle. Knit 2 together.

**RIGHT-LEANING TWISTED PURL DECREASE** Slip 1 knitwise. Slip another knitwise. Return the slipped stitches to the left needle. Purl 2 together.

**LEFT-LEANING TWISTED KNIT DECREASE** Insert the right needle from the right to the left into the back loops of 2 stitches. Knit them together.

**LEFT-LEANING TWISTED PURL DECREASE** Purl 2 together through the back loop.

# Chart

# Shape

| | RS: Knit |
| --- | --- |
| | WS: Purl |

| | RS: Knit through the back loop |
| --- | --- |
| | WS: Purl through the back loop |

| | RS: Purl through the back loop |
| --- | --- |
| | WS: Knit through the back loop |

| | RS: Right-leaning twisted knit decrease |
| --- | --- |
| | WS: Right-leaning twisted purl decrease |

| | RS: Left-leaning twisted knit decrease |
| --- | --- |
| | WS: Left-leaning twisted purl decrease |

| O | Yarn over |
| --- | --- |

| ↑ | Slip as if to purl |
| --- | --- |

| | Repeat these 16 rows until Curl reaches desired size. With each new repeat, work the yellow stitches 1 more time. |
| --- | --- |

# Merlinite

**SHOWN IN** Merino DK, a DK-weight yarn by Hedgehog Fibres, in the color Construct.

**GAUGE & SIZING** Shown at 20 stitches in 4 inches in pattern as charted. The piece shown used 500 yards of yarn and has a wingspan of 51 inches.

**CAST ON** Cast on 8 stitches.

**BODY** Odd rows are wrong-side rows. Even rows are right-side rows.

Work the Chart, repeating the 10 rows surrounded by the thick border as described in the key and note, until Curl reaches desired size. Each row increases the stitch count by 2. Stop after completing row 20 of the Chart.

Work the Finish Chart once. You'll repeat the 20 stitches surrounded by the purple border as needed to use up your stitches.

**FINISHING** Bind off loosely using a stretchy bind off. Weave in ends. Block to shape.

**NOTE** The 10 rows surrounded by the thick border are repeated to adjust the size of the Curl. The first time you work them, work the block of yellow stitches once. The second time you work them, work the block of yellow stitches 2 times. Each subsequent time you work them, work the block of yellow stitches 1 more time.

**RIGHT-LEANING TWISTED KNIT DECREASE** Slip 1 as if to purl. Remount the next stitch so it is rotated 180 degrees (one half turn) clockwise. Return the slipped stitch to the left needle. Knit 2 together.

**RIGHT-LEANING TWISTED PURL DECREASE** Slip 1 knitwise. Slip another knitwise. Return the slipped stitches to the left needle. Purl 2 together.

**LEFT-LEANING TWISTED KNIT DECREASE** Insert the right needle from the right to the left into the back loops of 2 stitches. Knit them together.

**LEFT-LEANING TWISTED PURL DECREASE** Purl 2 together through the back loop.

## Chart

| | RS: Knit / WS: Purl |
| | RS: Left-leaning twisted knit decrease / WS: Left-leaning twisted purl decrease |
| | RS: Right-leaning twisted knit decrease / WS: Right-leaning twisted purl decrease |
| | RS: Knit through the back loop / WS: Purl through the back loop |
| | Yarn over |
| | Slip as if to purl |
| | Repeat these 10 rows until Curl reaches desired size. With each new repeat, work the yellow stitches 1 more time. |
| | Repeat these 20 stitches as needed. |

## Shape

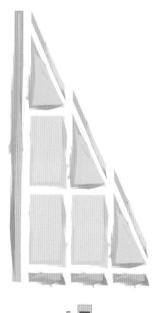

## Finish Chart

22

# Indicolite

**SHOWN IN** Squish DK, a DK-weight yarn by Spun Right Round, in the color Frost.

**GAUGE & SIZING** Shown at 22 stitches in 4 inches in pattern as charted. The piece shown used 550 yards of yarn and has a wingspan of 50 inches.

**CAST ON** Cast on 9 stitches.

**BODY** Odd rows are wrong-side rows. Even rows are right-side rows.

Work the Chart, repeating the 16 rows surrounded by the thick border as described in the key and note, until Curl reaches desired size. Each wrong-side row increases the stitch count by 1. Each right-side row increases the stitch count by 2. Stop after completing row 24 or 32 of the Chart.

Work the Finish Chart once. You'll repeat the 1 stitch surrounded by the purple border as needed to use up your stitches.

**FINISHING** Bind off loosely using a stretchy bind off. Weave in ends. Block to shape.

**NOTE** The 16 rows surrounded by the thick border are repeated to adjust the size of the Curl. The first time you work them, work the block of yellow stitches once. The second time you work them, work the block of yellow stitches 2 times. Each subsequent time you work them, work the block of yellow stitches 1 more time.

**SLIP 3 AS IF TO PURL** Slip 3 stitches as if to purl with the yarn held to the wrong side of your work.

**KNIT GRABBING THE STRANDS BELOW** Look on the back side of the curl and find the 3 strands of slipped stitches. Bring your right needle up under these 3 strands so they are sitting on your right needle. Knit the next stitch. Use your left needle to pass the 3 stitches over the stitch you just knit and off your needle.

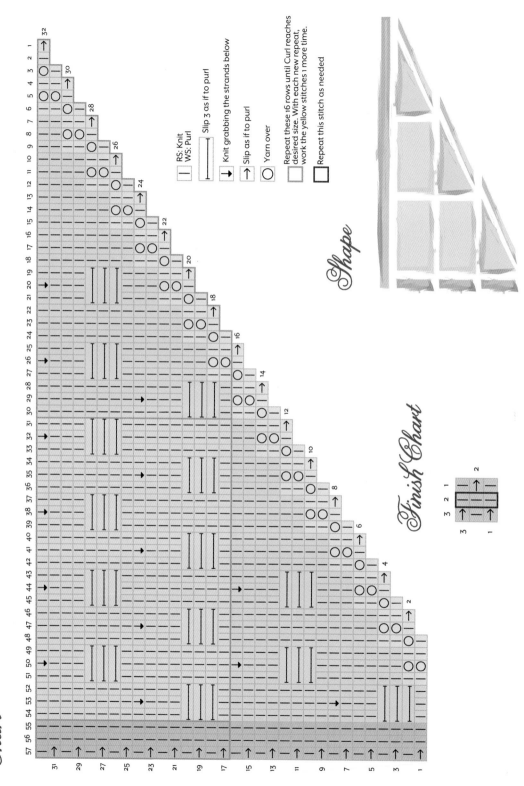

*Chart*

*Shape*

*Finish Chart*

| | | |
|---|---|---|
| RS: Knit | | |
| WS: Purl | | |
| | | Slip 3 as if to purl |
| | | Knit grabbing the strands below |
| | | Slip as if to purl |
| | | Yarn over |
| | | Repeat these 16 rows until Curl reaches desired size. With each new repeat, work the yellow stitches 1 more time. |
| | | Repeat this stitch as needed |

26

Charoite

**SHOWN IN** Tibetan Dream, a fingering-weight yarn by Bijou Spun, in the color Lavender Gradient Flow.

**GAUGE & SIZING** Shown at 32 stitches in 4 inches in pattern as charted. The piece shown used 625 yards of yarn and has a wingspan of 48 inches.

**CAST ON** Cast on 8 stitches.

**BODY** Odd rows are wrong-side rows. Even rows are right-side rows.

Work the Chart, repeating the 12 rows surrounded by the thick border as described in the key and note, until Curl reaches desired size. Each wrong-side row increases the stitch count by 1. Each right-side row increases the stitch count by 2. Stop after completing row 18 or 24 of the Chart.

Work the Finish Chart once. You'll repeat the 1 stitch surrounded by the purple border as needed to use up your stitches.

**FINISHING** Bind off loosely using a stretchy bind off. Weave in ends. Block to shape.

**NOTE** The 12 rows surrounded by the thick border are repeated to adjust the size of the Curl. The first time you work them, work the block of yellow stitches once. The second time you work them, work the block of yellow stitches 2 times. Each subsequent time you work them, work the block of yellow stitches 1 more time.

**3 X 3 CABLE LEFT** Slip 3 to cable needle, hold in front, knit 3, knit 3 from cable needle.

**3 X 3 CABLE RIGHT** Slip 3 to cable needle, hold in back, knit 3, knit 3 from cable needle.

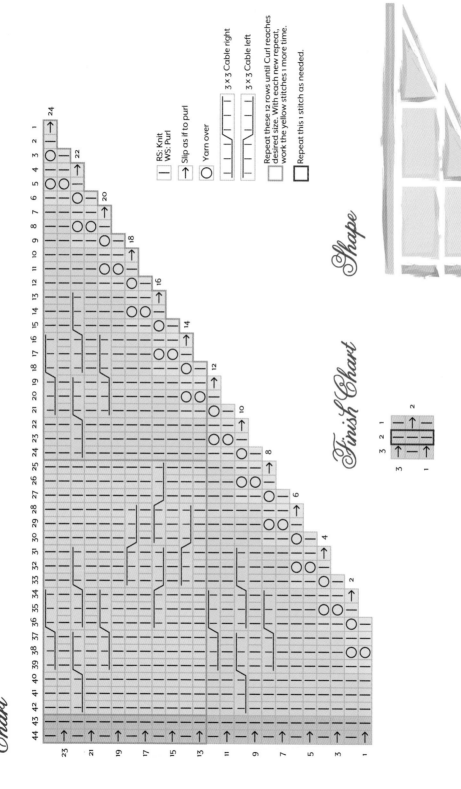

*Chart*

*Shape*

*Finish Chart*

RS: Knit
WS: Purl

↑ Slip as if to purl

○ Yarn over

3 x 3 Cable right

3 x 3 Cable left

Repeat these 12 rows until Curl reaches desired size. With each new repeat, work the yellow stitches 1 more time.

Repeat this 1 stitch as needed.

# Chalcopyrite

**SHOWN IN** Divine DK, a DK-weight yarn by Knitcircus, in the Brass and Steam gradient plus an extra skein of Brass Band, the yellow color at the end of Brass and Steam.

**GAUGE & SIZING** Shown at 20 stitches in 4 inches in pattern as charted. The piece shown used 525 yards of yarn and has a wingspan of 40 inches.

**CAST ON** Cast on 63 stitches.

**BODY** Note that the Chart is large and split across two pages to make sure the symbols are a reasonable size and easy to read.

Odd rows are right-side rows. Even rows are wrong-side rows.

Work the Chart, repeating the 20 rows surrounded by the thick border as described in the key and note, until Curl reaches desired size. Each right-side row increases the stitch count by 1. Each wrong-side row increases the stitch count by 2 (except row 20 which does not increase the stitch count). Stop after completing row 17 of the Chart (pay special attention here, you're not finishing the whole Chart, you're stopping after row 17).

Work the Finish Chart once (odd rows are wrong-side rows, even rows are right-side rows). You'll repeat the 14 stitches surrounded by the purple border as needed to use up your stitches.

**FINISHING** Bind off loosely using a stretchy bind off. Weave in ends. Block to shape.

**NOTE** The 20 rows surrounded by the thick border are repeated to adjust the size of the Curl. The first time you work them, work the block of yellow stitches once. The second time you work them, work the block of yellow stitches 2 times. Each subsequent time you work them, work the block of yellow stitches 1 more time.

**RIGHT-LEANING DOUBLE KNIT DECREASE** Slip 1 knitwise. Slip another knitwise. Return slipped stitches to the left needle. Insert the right needle from the right to the left into the back loops of both stitches and knit them together. Put the resulting stitch back on the left needle. Pass the second stitch on the left needle over the first. Slip the first stitch back to the right needle.

**LEFT-LEANING DOUBLE KNIT DECREASE** Slip 1 knitwise. Knit 2 together. Pass slipped stitch over.

**MAKE 1 RIGHT KNITWISE** With your left needle, lift the strand of yarn between the last stitch you worked and the stitch you would normally work next from the back to the front. Knit into the loop created by the strand of yarn you just picked up.

**MAKE 1 RIGHT PURLWISE** With your left needle, lift the strand of yarn between the last stitch you worked and the stitch you would normally work next from the back to the front. Purl into the loop created by the strand of yarn you just picked up.

**NO STITCH** This is just a placeholder to keep the chart lined up. You don't need to do anything, just move to the next square on the chart.

# Chart (left side: the chart spans two pages)

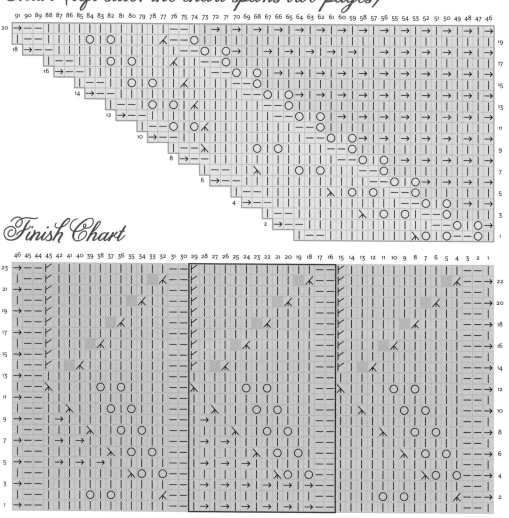

# Finish Chart

# Shape

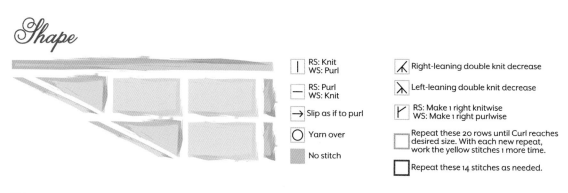

| | RS: Knit<br>WS: Purl | | Right-leaning double knit decrease |
| | RS: Purl<br>WS: Knit | | Left-leaning double knit decrease |
| → | Slip as if to purl | | RS: Make 1 right knitwise<br>WS: Make 1 right purlwise |
| O | Yarn over | | Repeat these 20 rows until Curl reaches desired size. With each new repeat, work the yellow stitches 1 more time. |
| | No stitch | | Repeat these 14 stitches as needed. |

# Chart (right side: the chart spans two pages)

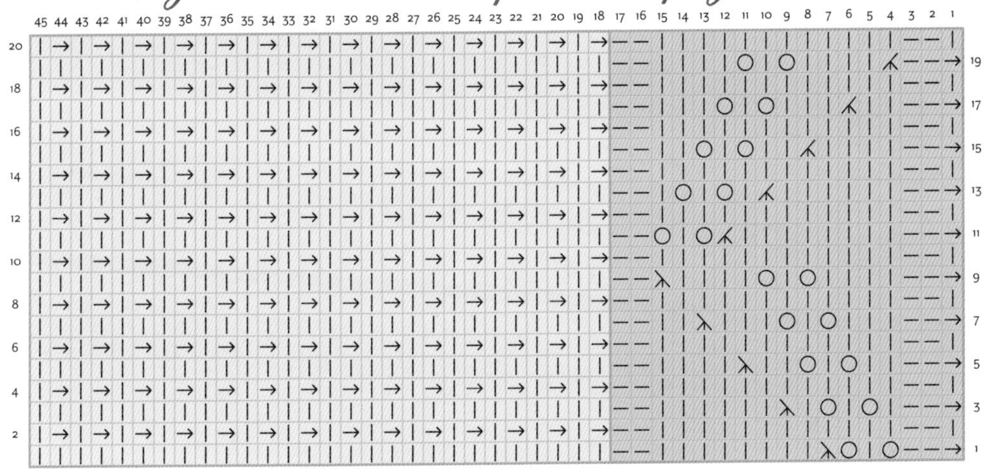


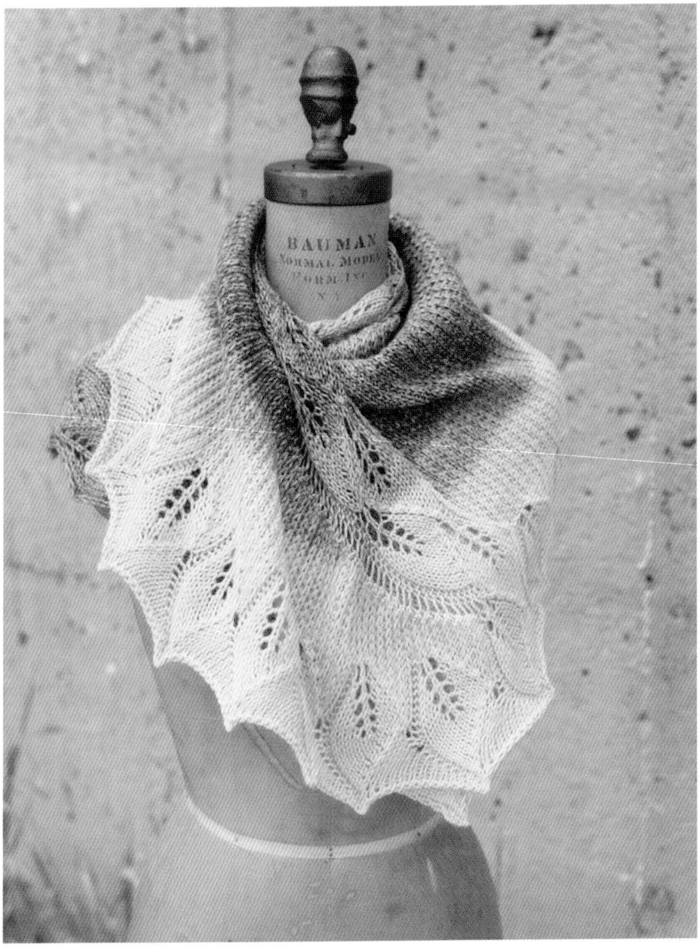

*Kyanite*

**SHOWN IN** Sojourn, a fingering-weight yarn by Miss Babs, in the color German Waterways (the piece shown used the four darkest blues and the gray from the set).

**GAUGE & SIZING** Shown at 24 stitches in 4 inches in pattern as charted. The piece shown used 800 yards of yarn and has a wingspan of 54 inches.

**CAST ON** Cast on 9 stitches.

**BODY** Odd rows are wrong-side rows. Even rows are right-side rows.

Work the Chart, repeating the 10 rows surrounded by the thick border as described in the key and note, changing colors as described in the Colors section, until Curl reaches desired size. Each wrong-side row increases the stitch count by 1. Each right-side row increases the stitch count by 2. Stop after completing row 10 of the Chart.

Work a final row by slipping the first stitch as if to purl and purling to the end.

**FINISHING** Bind off loosely using a stretchy bind off. Weave in ends. Block to shape.

**NOTE** The 10 rows surrounded by the thick border are repeated to adjust the size of the Curl. The first time you work them, work the block of yellow stitches once. The second time you work them, work the block of yellow stitches 16 times. Each subsequent time you work them, work the block of yellow stitches 15 more times.

**HORIZONTAL STITCH** Knit into the back loop of the second stitch on your left needle and leave that stitch on your needle. Knit into the back loop of the first stitch on your left needle. Let both the first and second stitch slide off your left needle. Slip the first stitch on your right needle back onto your left needle.

# Shape

| | RS: Knit<br>WS: Purl |
| → | Slip as if to purl |
| ○ | Yarn over |
| ← | Horizontal stitch |
| ☐ | Repeat these 10 rows until Curl reaches desired size. With each new repeat, work the yellow stitches 15 more times. |

# Chart

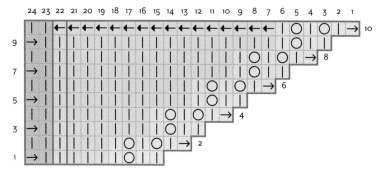

# Colors

**ROWS 1-8:** Main Color

**ROWS 9-10:** Accent Color

This Curl uses approximately equal amounts of five colors (light, medium, darker, and darkest shades of one color, plus an accent color). The accent color is the limiting yarn (the one you'll run out of first).

The four shades of the same color cycle through in turn with the accent color used between them.

- First use the *light* shade for rows 1-8, the *accent* for rows 9-10.

- Then use the *medium* shade for rows 1-8, the *accent* for rows 9-10.

- Then use the *darker* shade for rows 1-8, the *accent* for rows 9-10.

- Finally use the *darkest* shade for rows 1-8, the *accent* for rows 9-10.

Repeat until the Curl reaches the desired size.

You can easily use more shades of your color if you want (in which case you will definitely need more of the accent color than of each individual shade of color).

Zincite

**SHOWN IN** Chameleon Sock Tornadoz gradient set, a fingering-weight yarn by Indigodragonfly, in the color Cahoots.

**GAUGE & SIZING** Shown at 28 stitches in 4 inches in pattern as charted. The piece shown used 675 yards of yarn and has a wingspan of 53 inches.

**CAST ON** Cast on 22 stitches.

**BODY** Odd rows are wrong-side rows. Even rows are right-side rows.

Work the Chart, repeating the 12 rows surrounded by the thick border as described in the key and note, changing colors as described in the Colors section, until Curl reaches desired size. Each row increases the stitch count by 1 (except rows 11 and 12 which increase the stitch count by 2). Stop after completing row 12 of the Chart.

Work the Finish Chart once. You'll repeat the 1 stitch surrounded by the purple border as needed to use up your stitches.

**FINISHING** Bind off loosely using a stretchy bind off. Weave in ends. Block to shape.

**NOTE** The 12 rows surrounded by the thick border are repeated to adjust the size of the Curl. The first time you work them, work the block of yellow stitches once. The second time you work them, work the block of yellow stitches 2 times. Each subsequent time you work them, work the block of yellow stitches 1 more time.

**CENTERED DOUBLE KNIT DECREASE** Slip 2 together at the same time as if to knit 2 together. Knit 1. Pass the slipped stitches over.

**CENTERED DOUBLE PURL DECREASE** Slip 2 together at the same time as if to purl 2 together through the back loop (that means swing your right needle tip around behind your fabric and come into those two stitches from the left). Purl 1. Pass the slipped stitches over.

**LEFT-LEANING PURL DECREASE** Slip 1 knitwise. Slip another knitwise. Return slipped stitches to left needle. Purl 2 together through the back loops.

# Shape

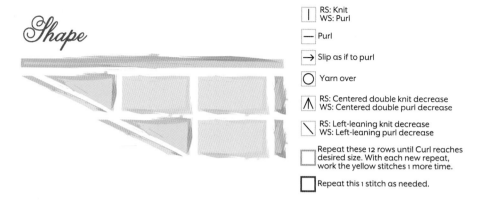

| | RS: Knit<br>WS: Purl |
|---|---|
| — | Purl |
| → | Slip as if to purl |
| O | Yarn over |
| /\ | RS: Centered double knit decrease<br>WS: Centered double purl decrease |
| \ | RS: Left-leaning knit decrease<br>WS: Left-leaning purl decrease |
| ☐ | Repeat these 12 rows until Curl reaches desired size. With each new repeat, work the yellow stitches 1 more time. |
| ☐ | Repeat this 1 stitch as needed. |

# Chart

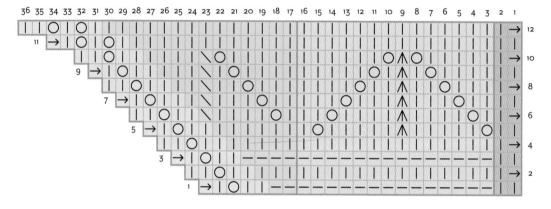

# Finish Chart

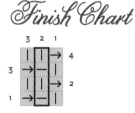

# Colors

This Curl uses approximately equal amounts of five colors. They cycle through in turn.

Work through rows 1-12 with the first color, then the second, then the third, then the fourth, then the fifth.

Repeat until the Curl reaches the desired size.

Work the Finish Chart in whatever color comes next in the progression.

You can easily use more colors if you want (just cycle through each color in turn)

Apatite

**SHOWN IN** Meridian, a fingering-weight yarn by Seven Sisters Arts, in the Water Garden gradient set.

**GAUGE & SIZING** Shown at 26 stitches in 4 inches in pattern as charted. The piece shown used 1,150 yards of yarn and has a wingspan of 72 inches.

**CAST ON** Cast on 8 stitches.

**BODY** Odd rows are right-side rows. Even rows are wrong-side rows.

Work the Chart, repeating the 8 rows surrounded by the thick border as described in the key and note, changing colors as described in the Colors section, until Curl reaches desired size. Each right-side row increases the stitch count by 1. Each wrong-side row increases the stitch count by 2. Stop after completing row 16 of the Chart.

Work a final row by slipping the first stitch as if to purl and knitting to the end.

**FINISHING** Bind off loosely using a stretchy bind off. Weave in ends. Block to shape.

**NOTE** The 8 rows surrounded by the thick border are repeated to adjust the size of the Curl. The first time you work them, work the block of yellow stitches once. The second time you work them, work the block of yellow stitches 2 times. Each subsequent time you work them, work the block of yellow stitches 1 more time.

**KNIT WRAPPING THE YARN 3 TIMES** Make a knit stitch, but wrap the yarn around the needle 3 times instead of once.

**CLUSTER** Slip 3 stitches to your right needle purlwise (letting the extra loops of yarn from the previous row drop off as you do). Put those stitches back on your left needle. Knit into the back loop of all 3 stitches at once but don't take them off the needle, yarn over, knit into the back loop of all 3 stitches at once and take the stitches off the needle.

# Shape

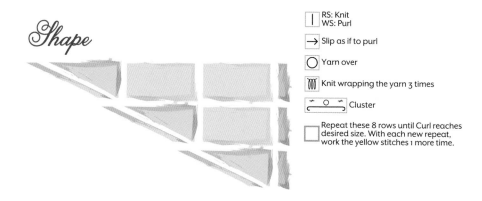

| | RS: Knit / WS: Purl |
| → | Slip as if to purl |
| O | Yarn over |
| ⦚⦚⦚ | Knit wrapping the yarn 3 times |
| ⌒O⌒ | Cluster |
| ☐ | Repeat these 8 rows until Curl reaches desired size. With each new repeat, work the yellow stitches 1 more time. |

# Chart

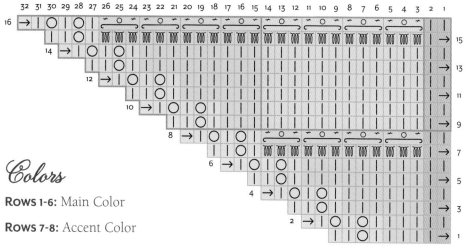

# Colors

**ROWS 1-6:** Main Color

**ROWS 7-8:** Accent Color

**ROWS 9-14:** Main Color

**ROWS 15-16:** Accent Color

This Curl uses approximately equal amounts of 3 shades of the same color (light, medium, and dark).

First, the light color is used as the main color, and the medium is used as the accent. Then the medium color is used as the main color and the dark used as the accent. Finally the dark color is used as the background and the light used as the accent.

- Use the light color as main and the medium color as accent until you've used one third of the light color.

- Use the medium color as main and the dark color as accent until you've used all the medium color or half the dark color, whichever comes first.

- Use the dark color as main and the light color as accent until you run out of either (leave enough to work the bind off with the dark color).

# Rhodonite

**SHOWN IN** Sublime DK, a DK-weight yarn by Black Trillium Fibres, in the Orchid gradient set.

**GAUGE & SIZING** Shown at 24 stitches in 4 inches in pattern as charted. The piece shown used 475 yards of yarn and has a wingspan of 44 inches.

**CAST ON** Cast on 31 stitches.

**BODY** Odd rows are wrong-side rows. Even rows are right-side rows.

Work the Chart, repeating the 12 rows surrounded by the thick border as described in the key and note, changing colors as described in the Colors section, until Curl reaches desired size. Each row increases the stitch count by 2. Stop after completing row 12 of the Chart.

Work a final row by slipping the first stitch as if to purl and purling to the end.

**FINISHING** Bind off loosely using a stretchy bind off. Weave in ends. Block to shape.

**NOTE** The 12 rows surrounded by the thick border are repeated to adjust the size of the Curl. The first time you work them, work the block of yellow stitches once. The second time you work them, work the block of yellow stitches 2 times. Each subsequent time you work them, work the block of yellow stitches 1 more time.

**LEFT-LEANING TWISTED KNIT DECREASE** Insert the right needle from the right to the left into the back loops of 2 stitches. Knit them together.

**CENTERED TWISTED DOUBLE KNIT DECREASE** Slip 1 as if to purl. Remount the next stitch so it is rotated 180 degrees (one half turn) clockwise. Return the slipped stitch to the left needle. Slip 2 together at the same time as if to knit 2 together. Knit 1. Pass the slipped stitches over.

## Chart

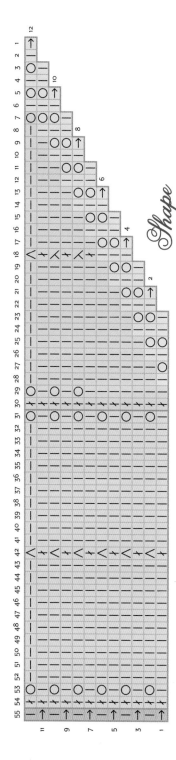

## Shape

## Legend

| | RS: Knit / WS: Purl |
| ↟ | RS: Knit through the back loop / WS: Purl through the back loop |
| — | Purl |
| ↑ | Slip as if to purl |
| O | Yarn over |
| ⟋ | Left-leaning twisted knit decrease |
| ⋀ | Centered twisted double knit decrease |
| ☐ | Repeat these 12 rows until Curl reaches desired size. With each new repeat, work the yellow stitches 1 more time. |

## Colors

**Rows 1-10:** Fat stripe

**Rows 11-12:** Thin stripe

This Curl uses approximately equal amounts of five colors (lightest, light, medium, dark, darkest shades of one color).

Work a fat stripe (rows 1-10), then a thin stripe (rows 11-12), and cycle through the colors (from lightest to darkest) on each stripe.

- First use the *lightest* shade for rows 1-10, the *dark* shade for rows 11-12.

- Then use the *light* shade for rows 1-10, the *darkest* shade for rows 11-12.

- Then use the *medium* shade for rows 1-10, the *lightest* shade for rows 11-12.

- Then use the *dark* shade for rows 1-10, the *light* shade for rows 11-12.

- Finally use the *darkest* shade for rows 1-10, the *medium* shade for rows 11-12.

Repeat until the Curl reaches the desired size. Work the bind off in the next color in the progression.

50

Cacoxenite

**SHOWN IN** Cheshire Cat, a fingering-weight yarn by Wonderland Yarns, in the color Goat's Beard as the background and Yellow to Fuscia Shadow #41 Color Morph as the accent.

**GAUGE & SIZING** Shown at 24 stitches in 4 inches in pattern as charted. The piece shown used 550 yards of yarn and has a wingspan of 60 inches.

**CAST ON** Cast on 19 stitches.

**BODY** Note that the Chart is large and split across two pages to make sure the symbols are a reasonable size and easy to read.

Odd rows are right-side rows. Even rows are wrong-side rows.

Work the Chart, repeating the 40 rows surrounded by the thick border as described in the key and note, changing colors as described in the Colors section, until Curl reaches desired size. Each wrong-side row increases the stitch count by 2. Each right-side row increases the stitch count by 1. Stop after completing row 8 or 16 or 24 or 32 or 40 of the Chart.

Work the Finish Chart once. You'll repeat the 1 stitch surrounded by the purple border as needed to use up your stitches.

**FINISHING** Bind off loosely using a stretchy bind off. Weave in ends. Block to shape.

**NOTE** The 40 rows surrounded by the thick border are repeated to adjust the size of the Curl. The first time you work them, work the block of yellow stitches once. The second time you work them, work the block of yellow stitches 7 times. Each subsequent time you work them, work the block of yellow stitches 6 more time.

**PURL WRAPPING THE YARN 2 TIMES** Make a purl stitch, but wrap the yarn around the needle 2 times instead of once. Drop the extra loop when you come to this stitch on the next row.

# Chart (left side: remember, the chart spans two pages)

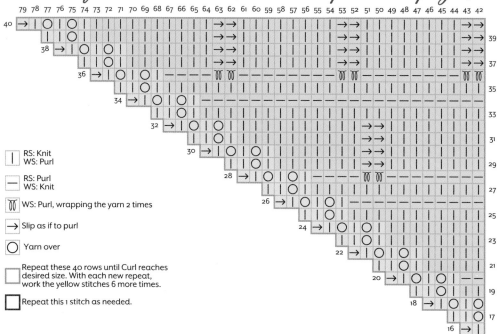

**Legend:**

| RS: Knit WS: Purl |
| RS: Purl WS: Knit |
| WS: Purl, wrapping the yarn 2 times |
| Slip as if to purl |
| Yarn over |
| Repeat these 40 rows until Curl reaches desired size. With each new repeat, work the yellow stitches 6 more times. |
| Repeat this 1 stitch as needed. |

## Colors

**ROWS 1-4, 9-12, 17-20, 25-28, 33-36:** Main Color

**ROWS 5-8, 13-16, 21-24, 29-32, 37-40:** Accent Color

This Curl has a background color and five accent colors (A, B, C, D, and E). The background color is about half the total yardage, and each of the accent colors is about one tenth the total yardage.

Work 4 rows with the background color, then four rows with an accent color. Repeat, cycling through each accent color in turn.

- Use the *background* color for rows 1-4, then *accent A* for rows 5-8.

## Finish Chart

- Use the *background* color for rows 9-12, then *accent B* for rows 13-16.

- Use the *background* color for rows 17-20, then *accent C* for rows 21-24.

- Use the *background* color for rows 25-28, then *accent D* for rows 29-32.

- Use the *background* color for rows 33-36, then *accent E* for rows 37-40.

Repeat until the Curl reaches the desired size. Work the Finish Chart in the *background* color.

# Chart (right side: remember, the chart spans two pages)

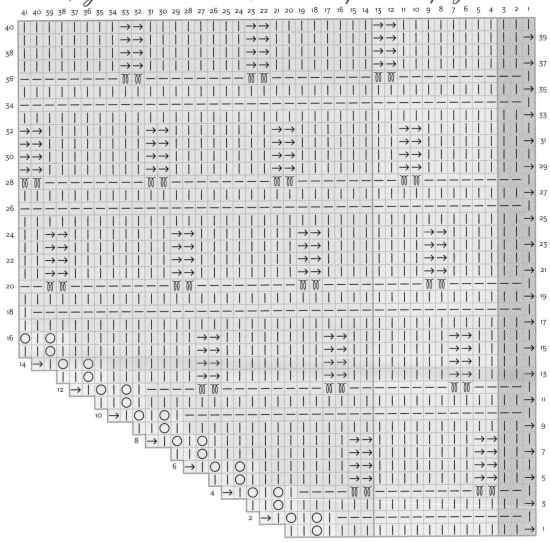

# Shape

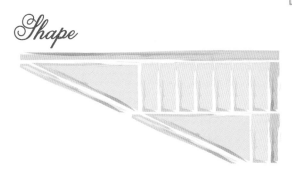

# Thanks

My name on the cover? It's a bit of a lie. It makes it look like I'm doing this all by myself. The reality is that this is totally a team project. I could never do this alone!

My sample knitters are my secret weapon. Katie Metzroth, Ellen Cooper, and Barbara Stephenson are all absolute magicians and work wonders with their needles. I send them notes and yarn (and a frankly alarming number of text messages and emails), and they send me back helpful suggestions and staggeringly perfect knitting. They made all the pieces you see here, and there wouldn't be a book without them.

But books need more than just pretty knitting to fill their pages. You've got to get some words and charts in there, too. Cathy Scott and Heather Ordover make sure those bits behave themselves. Cathy (the superstar responsible for the fabulous Stitchmastery Knitting Chart Editor I use for all my charts) edited the patterns. When your knitting goes smoothly, it's totally her doing. And Heather (creator of the marvelous CraftLit podcast, and all around crafty mastermind) made sure the words that end up on the page actually said what I thought they said. When it sounds like I know what I'm talking about, that's totally her doing.

And while those folks were busy taking care of the knitting and the words, there were other people busy taking care of me. My parents continued to send me pictures of themselves posing in yarn shops with my books (doubtless to the amusement of the yarn shop owners). Lana Holden reminded me that "it's all crap, everything I make is crap, I should just quit before everyone finds out" is actually a standard stage in the book making process and not an accurate assessment of the situation. Brian Glenn cheerfully squandered two perfectly good weekend mornings hunting for decrepit walls to take pictures in front of, tried once again to explain hyphens to me, and quietly set lunch (and occasionally dinner) in front of me when I had one-second-I'm-writing face for a week straight there at the end.

The secret really is having a team, and my team is awesome!

# Sources

Feel free to substitute yarns. Just know that if you use a different weight of yarn or make your Curl a different size, you will almost certainly need a different amount of yarn.

**CHARTS** were created with Stitchmastery Knitting Chart Editor.
**STITCHMASTERY.COM**

**BLOCKING WIRES** from Inspinknity.
**INSPINKNITY.COM**

**HOWLITE** uses about 725 yards of Daintree by Skein. Fingering weight, 65% superwash merino, 20% bamboo, 15% silk.
**SKEINYARN.COM**

**LEPIDOLITE** uses about 650 yards of Silky Victoria by Blue Moon Fiber Arts. Sport weight, 85% polwarth, 15% silk.
**BLUEMOONFIBERARTS.COM**

**MERLINITE** uses about 500 yards of Merino DK by Hedgehog Fibres. DK weight, 100% superwash merino.
**HEDGEHOGFIBRES.COM**

**INDICOLITE** uses about 500 yards of Squish DK by Spun Right Round. DK weight, 100% superwash merino.
**SPUNRIGHTROUND.COM**

**CHAROITE** uses about 625 yards of Tibetan Dream by Bijou Spun. Fingering weight, 85% yak, 15% nylon.
**BIJOUBASINRANCH.COM**

**CHALCOPYRITE** uses about 525 yards of Divine DK by Knitcircus. DK weight, 100% superwash merino.
**KNITCIRCUS.COM**

**ZINCITE** uses about 675 yards of Chameleon Sock Tornadoz gradient set by Indigodragonfly. Fingering weight, 63% superwash merino, 20% cashmere, 17% silk.
**INDIGODRAGONFLY.CA**

**APATITE** uses about 1,150 yards of Meridian by Seven Sisters Arts. Fingering weight, 75% superwash merino, 25% nylon.
**SEVENSISTERSARTS.COM**

**RHODONITE** uses about 475 yards of Sublime DK by Black Trillium Fibres. DK weight, 100% superwash merino.
**BLACKTRILLIUMFIBRES.COM**

**CACOXENITE** uses about 550 yards of Cheshire Cat by Wonderland Yarns. Fingering weight, 100% superwash merino.
**BLACKTRILLIUMFIBRES.COM**

# Other Works

So this book thing? It turns out it's awfully addictive! These are some of the books I've published so far. But I seem to have made something of a habit of this, so I can just about promise there will be more soon.

If you want to see what's in these books, find out what else might have shown up recently, or just see what I'm up to, visit **PANTSVILLEPRESS.COM**.

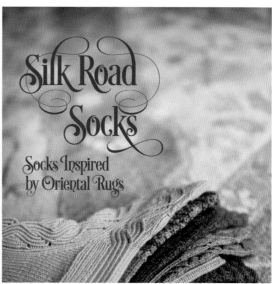

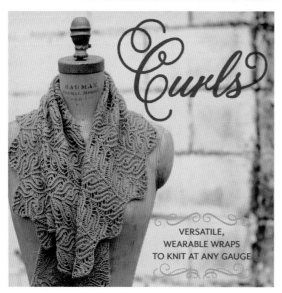